MW00379280

Healing
RELATIONSHIPS

What if Forgiveness and Repentance
Aren't What You Think They Are?

A FOUR-PART GROUP STUDY

Healing Relationships
Copyright 2021 Trueface

All Rights Reserved. No part of **Healing Relationships** may be reproduced, stored in a retrieval system, or transmitted, in any form or in any means—by electronic, mechanical, photocopying, recording or otherwise—in any form without permission. Thank you for buying an authorized edition of this book and for complying with copyright laws.

Scripture quotations marked (NIV) are taken from the Holy Bible, New International Version®, NIV®. Copyright © 1973, 1978, 1984, 2011 by Biblica, Inc.™

Scripture quotations marked (NLT) are taken from the Holy Bible, New Living Translation, copyright © 1996, 2004, 2007 by Tyndale House Foundation. Used by permission of Tyndale House Publishers, Inc., Carol Stream, Illinois 60188. All rights reserved.

Scripture quotations marked (ESV) are from The Holy Bible, English Standard Version® (ESV®), copyright © 2001 by Crossway, *a publishing ministry of Good News Publishers. Used by permission. All right reserved.*

Scripture quotations marked (NASB) are taken from the NEW AMERICAN STANDARD BIBLE®, Copyright ©1960, 1962, 1963, 1968, 1971, 1973, 1975, 1977, 1995 by The Lockman Foundation. Used by permission.

Cover & Interior Design by Outskirts Studio

Produced by **Trueface**
Trueface.org
ISBN: 978-1-7348805-1-9

Printed in the United States.

CONTENTS

GETTING STARTED

Welcome to *Healing Relationships*! We all experience broken relationships throughout our lives. From short-lived fights with a friend to a decade-long silence between family members, these fractures cause deep pain in our lives. They hurt because we were made for authentic and abiding relationships. As followers of Jesus, we are called to pursue healing in these relationships (Matthew 5:23-25), standing against the division and isolation that so often follows conflict (Romans 12:17-21). This study is designed to help you experience relational healing in your life as you participate in God's Kingdom of love, justice, and reconciliation.

2 Corinthians 5:17-19 (NIV)

"Therefore, if anyone is in Christ, the new creation has come: The old has gone, the new is here! All this is from God, who reconciled us to himself through Christ and gave us the ministry of reconciliation: that God was reconciling the world to himself in Christ, not counting people's sins against them. And he has committed to us the message of reconciliation."

You can find all the session videos and additional resources at **trueface.org/HealingRelationshipsStudy**. Simply sign up for a free account and choose the *Healing Relationships* course.

Healing Relationships is structured similarly to other Trueface studies, which means that within each meeting you will go through three sections:

CONNECT

Spend time connecting with each other in order to deepen relationships.

LEARN

Use content to learn and grow spiritually.

LIVE

Discuss and apply what you learned to your here-and-now lives so that you can live out and experience these truths.

HOW TO FACILITATE: We have provided recommended time frames to help you stay on track in your meetings. These time frames reference a sixty- or ninety-minute group meeting.

TRUEFACE

beyond the mask

Today's culture is perfecting the art and science of creating masks. Behind these masks, people are dying inside. We're here to change that.

Trueface equips people to experience the freedom of living beyond the mask, because behind the mask is the real you. When we increase trust in our relationships, we are able to experience being more authentically known and loved by God and others.

We hope to be a bridge for hundreds of thousands to experience the peace and freedom of the original good news by trusting God and others with their whole selves . . . the self behind the mask.

To learn more about Trueface, visit *trueface.org*, or join the thousands of people living the Trueface life on social media.

Instagram: @truefacelife

Facebook: @truefacecommunity

Twitter: @truefaced

Trueface is a non-profit supported by people who have been impacted by the ministry. To help us create more resources like this one, visit *trueface.org/give.*

LOGISTICS

You'll find the videos and other additional resources for this study at *trueface.org/HealingRelationshipsStudy.* The videos and resources are free to use and are broken up by each meeting. Simply create a free account and sign up for the *Healing Relationships* course to get access to this content.

Below is a place for you to write down when you'll meet, where you'll meet, and the most important thing—who'll bring the food! Fill out this section with your group members in your first meeting.

MEETING 1:

Called to Be Peacemakers

Date:_____

Location: _____

Snacks:_____

MEETING 2:

God's Gift of Healing

Date:_____

Location: _____

Snacks:_____

MEETING 3:

Healing Starts With Me and God

Date:_____

Location: _____

Snacks:_____

MEETING 4:

Healing Overflows to You and Me

Date:_____

Location: _____

Snacks:_____

WEEK 1

Called to Be Peacemakers

MEETING TOGETHER

Have someone read this out loud:

Welcome to Healing Relationships! While our stories might be different, we have all experienced the pain of broken relationships—whether we hurt someone, or someone hurt us. It can be tempting to let those relationships fade away or try to pretend what happened wasn't a big deal, but that strategy doesn't work. We continue to experience pain and miss out on the peace and freedom that Jesus makes possible.

In this study we'll explore God's path to relational healing, joining him in the ministry of reconciliation, love, and healing. This is how we help usher the Kingdom of God into our own lives and communities.

This first week we'll talk about why these broken relationships are a big deal, why it's so tricky to navigate forgiveness and repentance, and where trust comes into this experience.

NOTES

CONNECT

🕐 **THIS SECTION WILL TAKE ABOUT** 30% **OF YOUR TIME TOGETHER TODAY.**

AS A GROUP:

- Pray:

    » Have someone pray to open this study. Invite the Holy Spirit to prepare your hearts to experience more of God's love and grace.

- Connect questions:

    » Think about your childhood years. Who did you not like, and why didn't you like them? Who did you really like, and why?

    » What hopes and/or concerns do you have for doing this study?

LEARN

🕐 **THIS SECTION WILL TAKE ABOUT** 20% **OF YOUR TIME TOGETHER TODAY.**

 WATCH THE *ROUNDTABLE* VIDEO.
Find at ***trueface.org/HealingRelationshipsStudy.***

NOTES

LIVE

◑ **THIS SECTION WILL TAKE ABOUT 50% OF YOUR TIME TOGETHER TODAY.**

In these "Live" sections, you will typically spend about half of your time on discussion, and half of your time on application.

REFLECT:

Have someone read the following passage out loud:

James 3:17-18 (NIV)

"But the wisdom that comes from heaven is first of all pure; then peace-loving, considerate, submissive, full of mercy and good fruit, impartial and sincere. Peacemakers who sow in peace raise a harvest of righteousness."

Then, spend one minute in silence individually as you pray this prayer:

God, where do you want to bring relational healing in my life?

NOTES

DISCUSS:

What does this mean to me?

After you watch the video, **choose a few questions** from the list below to process together. You don't need to get through all of them. It can be tempting to give the "right" or "expected" answer for these questions. Resist that urge! Try to be as honest and real as you can.

1. What stood out to you from the video?

2. What do you think is the difference between peacekeeping and peacemaking?

3. Why would the enemy want to break us apart and keep us apart?

4. When conflict comes up in a relationship, what's your go-to response? Pretend it didn't happen, seek out reconciliation, downplay the situation, blame the other person, or something else?

5. Keisha shared how she didn't feel seen by her community and how hurtful that was—and how it was harder to express her hurt than simply re-define her relationships. When have you experienced this?

6. How should following Jesus change our response to broken relationships? Read 1 Peter 3:8-11 and process together.

7. When you think of broken relationships in your own life, who is the first person that comes to mind?

NOTES

APPLY:

What faith step is God inviting me to take?

As followers of Jesus we are called to let his truth
and grace transform our lives. It can be tempting to
talk about healing without letting it change our actual
relationships. It's a lot easier to have an intellectual
discussion about the concept of forgiveness than to
have a messy, difficult conversation with someone
who has deeply hurt us. But when we don't let Jesus's
teachings change our here-and-now lives, we miss
out on the true joy, freedom, and abounding love
that he makes possible. Spend some time as a group
discussing how to step out in applying relational
healing in your own life.

- What is one practical, tangible way you can move
  towards relational healing this week? Some ideas
  are below:

  » Set aside time to revisit our prayer from
    earlier: *God, where do you want to bring
    relational healing in my life?*

  » Write out anyone that comes to mind that you
    feel you need to experience relational healing
    with, and then write out what barriers are
    preventing you from moving forward.

  » If it is safe, reach out to someone you are
    experiencing conflict with simply to touch
    base and invest in that relationship.

» Spend some time considering what you saw as conflict management growing up. What did it teach you about responding to conflict, good or bad?

» Pay attention to any fractures, big or small, in your relationships this next week. This might be at home, work, with friends, or somewhere else. How can you pursue healing in those moments?

» Does anything else come to mind? Be creative, but practical. Try to make it an actionable step in order to help integrate your actions with your beliefs.

• How I'm going to live it out (writing it down will help you remember it!):

• How can the group come alongside you over the next week? Letting other people love, encourage, and walk with you is a foundational piece of any grace-filled relationship.

NOTES

NOTES

- Look ahead to the Digging Deeper 1 material, where we begin digging into the anatomy of sin and what's happening underneath these conflicts. There are five sections for you to read through between now and your next meeting. If you don't get to them, that's okay. You won't get as much time to process in this study, but don't let that keep you from engaging in your group.

PRAY TO CLOSE OUT THIS TIME TOGETHER.

01

DIGGING DEEPER

Between now and your next meeting, read these five sections and reflect on the questions at the end. You can do them all at once, but we suggest breaking the five sections over multiple days to give yourself more processing time. This week we will explore the anatomy of sin and its effects in our lives.

If you are not able to go through the five sections before your next meeting, **that's okay**. Don't let it stop you from connecting with your community.

PASSAGE FOR THE WEEK

Psalm 51:1-2 (NLT)

"Have mercy on me, O God,
because of your unfailing love.
Because of your great compassion,
blot out the stain of my sins.
Wash me clean from my guilt.
Purify me from my sin."

SECTION 1

In the very beginning of humanity's story, God declares that it is not good for man to be alone. We were made for relationships, and we see this on a biological, emotional, and spiritual level. Humans flourish in the context of rich, authentic, healthy relationships with God and with others, and the result is an outpouring of love, justice, mercy, creativity, compassion, joy, courage, wisdom, and so much more.

Our relationships are an essential tool for the enemy in the war that he wages. We are too powerful when we are truly with and for each other. We protect, encourage, remind, and love one another. So he breaks us apart.

We all have had a painful experience of broken or bruised relationships, whether our mind goes to a friend, family member, coworker, spouse, mentor, or someone else. Inevitably, our rough edges collide with

NOTES

someone else's and relational pain is the result. We sometimes inflict it. Sometimes we have it inflicted on us. Often, it will be a little bit of both. While it can be tempting to just cut ties and go our separate ways, over time this weakens all our relationships. We learn that our relationships will only last until there is conflict. This leaves us either holding ourselves at a distance out of protection, or desperately trying to avoid any friction. Neither of these lead to fulfilling, trustworthy relationships. God made us for relationships that can not only weather conflict but can actually grow stronger and closer because of it.

God has designed us to be aware of these fractures and to know when something has gone wrong in a relationship. When someone sins against us, our involuntary response is *hurt*. This is our natural, human response—we don't have to work to create it. If we get punched in the gut, we pitch forward. If we touch a pan that's hot, we snatch our hand back from the stove. If we are sinned against, our hearts recoil with hurt.

This isn't a bad thing! This is a holy, helpful, beautiful warning bell that something needs to be addressed with the other person. Unfortunately, many of us have been taught that this *is* a bad thing. We "shouldn't" feel hurt. Maybe we've been told we're being too sensitive. Maybe we've learned that admitting we're hurt is a sign of weakness. Maybe we were taught that we should go along with what anyone else wanted and not rock the boat—which definitely means not admitting when we're hurt. Or, on the flip side, some

NOTES

19

NOTES

of us learned that expressing our hurt was a way to control others. We learned to use it as a weapon to get our way, make someone else do what we want, or avoid facing a hard truth. Many of us struggle to acknowledge our hurt in a healthy way.

The problem is that when we ignore our hurt, either by avoiding it or turning it into a weapon, it doesn't disappear. We put it in a drawer and pretend like it's not there, but it's alive and well. And left alone, our hurt grows and mutates. By the time we encounter it again it's often an unrecognizable monster, and we find ourselves at a loss as to where it came from. The first monster it turns into is shame, a deep-seated feeling that something is wrong with our very self. We believe we were hurt because there's something uniquely wrong with us. This is the inevitable effect of sin left untreated in our lives—even when it's sin performed against us.

Shame can present itself in a lot of different ways when it comes from hurt, including:

- bitterness
- anger
- self-protection
- blame
- suspicion
- control

- insecurity
- arrogance
- denial
- withdrawal
- avoidance
- isolation

. . . and many more. We have ignored the natural signals that we need relational healing, and now we have seemingly unrelated symptoms that are as confusing to us as they are to others.

Jesus knew that we would need a way home from this spiraling series of events. When we have been hurt, the way home is called forgiveness. It can be a challenging road, but it's a beautiful one too. There may be a lot of thoughts that run through our head about forgiveness: how it's been modeled to us, when it's been demanded of us, or perhaps how it has even been used against us. This study will guide us along a path of forgiveness we may not have experienced before—a forgiveness that walks hand in hand with Jesus. This path provides peace and freedom, and forgiveness that feels like a gift instead of a duty. Forgiveness isn't about "letting someone off the hook" or pretending that something didn't happen. Forgiving someone doesn't mean we trust them again or are saying what they did is okay. Forgiveness is a gift for *our* benefit. It's Jesus's way to give us freedom from the sin done against us.

NOTES

SCRIPTURE

Psalm 147:3 (NIV)

"He heals the brokenhearted and binds up their wounds."

REFLECTION QUESTIONS

When you feel hurt, what do you do? Do you pretend it didn't hurt, stew on it, address it with the person, use it as a way to control the situation, or something else? (If the thought, "I never get hurt," just went through your mind, do you remember ever being hurt, maybe when you were younger? How did that go?)

When you read the list of some of the things hurt can mutate into, which ones did you connect with? If you asked those closest to you to be deeply honest, which have they experienced with you?

Ask the Holy Spirit to help you explore where you need to experience forgiveness. This could be with someone currently in your life or from many years ago. Trust the Spirit to bring something to mind, even if it's surprising to you.

SECTION 2

Our involuntary response to hurt has a twin: guilt. When we are the one that has hurt someone else and sinned against them, the signal that goes through our system is: "You have done something wrong." Just like hurt, we can deal with this in many different ways. We might go directly to the person we've hurt and seek forgiveness and restoration. Or, we pretend that what we've done wasn't a big deal, like the other person shouldn't feel hurt. Perhaps we over-exaggerate our guilt so that the other person ends up comforting *us* and we can avoid facing our behavior. Sometimes we just ignore it all together, putting it in the drawer next to our hurt and pretending it's not there.

But the story goes the same way. Sin left untreated does not go away. It does not slowly dissipate over time—instead, it grows in strength, transforming in the dark. Just like with hurt, our guilt first becomes shame. This latest sin proves that there is something uniquely wrong with us. We move from "I've done something wrong," to "I *am* wrong." "What kind of person would do that?" we think to ourselves. "An ugly, messed-up person. I can't let anyone see me like this." So, we cover up. We strengthen our defenses against feeling our guilt.

Just like before, the inevitable effects of shame are the same here with guilt as they were with hurt. Our shame shows up as anger, denial, isolation, self-protection, control, avoidance, insecurity, bitterness, blame, suspicion, arrogance, withdrawal, and more. We've ignored the Spirit's call to healing and repentance, and now are dealing with inevitable effects that often result in wounding others more. It's a vicious, painful cycle, and it is one we're often unaware of.

The road to relational healing when we've hurt someone else is called repentance, and it's surprisingly similar to forgiveness—difficult, beautiful, and traversed with Jesus by our side at all times.

We may have had repentance modeled to us in many different ways. Think of the kid that takes another child's toy, and the second child starts crying. The first kid's parent might admonish him, saying, "Now say you're sorry." The child may say the required words without feeling them, believing them, or even maybe knowing why he's saying them. Some of us never graduate from this point. We say we're sorry, but our experience of repentance is that it's a duty, a lip-service, a grit-your-teeth-and-do-it task, rather than a freeing gift. Others of us had caregivers who withdrew their love if we didn't apologize, and so now we repent out of a desire to gain back love and worth rather than out of sincere regret.

Many fears can come up when we approach genuine repentance. It feels like giving up control and laying down our defenses. We often don't want to feel the sting of how we've hurt someone else, so we protect and excuse and avoid. What is so difficult to imagine on this side of repentance is how freeing, healing, and joyful the other side can be. It is painful to acknowledge how we've hurt others, but the pain of letting sin mutate in the background of our lives is far, far worse. It's like the difference between breaking your arm and experiencing a slow cancer. One hurts terribly in the exact moment, but the other can take your life if left to grow.

Approaching repentance requires courage. Thankfully, we have a God who tells us, "And be sure of this: I am with you always, even to the end of the age." (Matthew 28:20, NLT). You do not have to walk this road by yourself. You are under the protection and guidance of a God who designed the path itself.

NOTES

SCRIPTURE

Psalm 32:5 (NIV)

"Then I acknowledged my sin to you
*   and did not cover up my iniquity.*
I said, 'I will confess
*   my transgressions to the Lord.'*
And you forgave
*   the guilt of my sin."*

REFLECTION QUESTIONS

When you feel that prick of guilt and know you've hurt another person, what is your knee-jerk defense mechanism? Do you immediately dive into shame ("What's wrong with me?"), minimize ("It's not a big deal"), avoid ("I'm just not going to think about it"), blame ("Well if they hadn't been so annoying, I wouldn't have lost my temper!"), turn the tables ("I feel so badly about hurting you, now comfort me!") or something else?

NOTES

When you use one of the above defense mechanisms, what are you defending? Your motivations, reputation, view of yourself, something else?

Does a different inevitable effect jump out at you in relation to guilt? Which ones?

- anger
- denial
- isolation
- self-protection
- control
- avoidance

- insecurity
- bitterness
- blame
- suspicion
- arrogance
- withdrawal

Ask the Holy Spirit where you need to experience repentance. Sometimes, these areas can be more hidden from us than areas where we need to forgive. Let the Spirit guide you as you consider who you may have hurt.

NOTES

SECTION 3

We've touched on shame the last two days, but let's look at it a little more closely. Shame is an incredibly powerful, quiet, deadly weapon of the enemy. It poisons us, keeps us isolated from each other, drives us to avoid the love of God and others, and tempts us to prove our worth at any cost. It is completely and utterly opposed to the purpose and power of the Kingdom of God.

Shame has been the enemy's weapon of choice from the beginning of humanity's story. After Adam and Eve ate the forbidden fruit, the very next verse is Genesis 3:7, "At that moment their eyes were opened, and they suddenly felt shame at their nakedness. So they sewed fig leaves together to cover themselves." (NLT). This shame, this belief not that "I have done something wrong," but that "there is something uniquely and fundamentally wrong *with* me," has followed us ever since.

One of the ways that we get in touch with the lies of shame is through examining our beliefs about our identity. When we look at our hearts, what do we see? Who do we think we are, truly? How do we speak to ourselves? What are we most afraid of others seeing if they got too close? We cannot experience the true relational healing Jesus offers us without addressing our shame. They are opposite processes. One invites us to step into the light and offer our true hearts. The other drives us to hide, protecting ourselves at all costs.

Our theology can really put us in a bind here. If we have grown up hearing the constant refrain of "You're a sinner," then that is how we will see our hearts. We're dirty, wretched beings who certainly should never come into the light or we'll scare the daylights out of everyone. On the other hand, if we listen to the constant refrain of the New Testament, which tells us, "You're a saint, who still sins," we will know that our new, Christ-fused hearts are beautiful, loved, pure, and holy. Do we still have flesh, with all its patterns and hang-ups and prolific ability to mess up? You bet. Is that *who we truly are?* Absolutely not.

If this is a new conversation for you, we encourage you to check out our study *Two Roads*, where we unpack this in far more depth. In order to enter into the kind of forgiveness and repentance Jesus made possible, we will have to acknowledge and allow Jesus to take care of our shame. Jesus died for both our sin *and our shame*, in order to give us a shame-free identity. This is not a one-and-done experience, but a constant conversation with Jesus as we allow him to tell us who we truly are, as opposed to who shame tries to tell us we are. Out of the strength and security of our identity in Christ, we can wade into the turbulent waters of true healing and reconciliation.

NOTES

29

SCRIPTURE

Hebrews 12:1-2 (NIV)

"Therefore, since we are surrounded by such a great cloud of witnesses, let us throw off everything that hinders and the sin that so easily entangles. And let us run with perseverance the race marked out for us, fixing our eyes on Jesus, the pioneer and perfecter of faith. For the joy set before him he endured the cross, scorning its shame, and sat down at the right hand of the throne of God."

REFLECTION QUESTIONS

When you imagine your heart laid bare for anyone to see, how do you feel? How would you envision that heart? Feel free to use the space below to draw it out if helpful.

Why is it so important to deal with shame if we want true relational healing? How does shame hinder our relationships?

NOTES

SECTION 4

UNFORGIVENESS

Let's explore what it can look like when we are hurt and do not enter into heartfelt forgiveness. Each situation is unique, but the process is remarkably similar when we do not allow Jesus to lead us into forgiveness.

You become preoccupied with the event.
You rehearse it over and over. You don't sleep well. Worse, you're devastated to discover the person who hurt you seems to be enjoying their life just fine, barely even able to remember the particulars of the event.

You become a prosecuting attorney, consistently building your case.
You now globalize accusations, often totally unrelated to the issue. You begin to rewrite the history of your relationship, repainting each memory into more proof that perhaps they might be a serial killer after all! Accumulated evidence mounts so high that you cannot possibly imagine any wrongdoing on your side. You forget that just because you're hurt, that doesn't mean you're right in every turn of the relationship.

You become obsessed with "justice and accuracy."
"Yes, but you said . . . !" You now have all the grace and flexibility of a warden. You judge motives, memorize exact words, demand payment, and call for swift and severe sentencing.

You become unable to love well, neglecting the needs of others.
You're so preoccupied with your self-defense that you become largely aloof to the normally clear indications of others who need your attention, care, and presence. These might be your children, spouse, friends, or others.

You become unable to see from any other vantage points but your own.
Your desperate need to hear the other's groveling repentance makes you rigid against seeing possible other motivations causing this event. Whatever wrong you may have done since then can be deflected as logical necessity from this incredible injustice.

You become more and more uptight until your joy is robbed.
Until justice happens, the judge, attorneys, jury, bailiff, and stenographers are not allowed to go home. Between the incessant rehearsing of your side of the story and your vigilant gathering of evidence, you're about as fun as a clerk at the DMV.

You become progressively more unhealthy.
Growing bitterness makes you irrational, overbearing, hyper-sensitive, angry, and petty. It is hard even for friends to be around you for extended periods. You're not a safe person.

You become intent on telling "your side of things" to as many as possible.
Eventually, almost everyone you know is poisoned with your distorted, thinly veiled character assassinations.

You become unable to interpret history accurately.
Though you can quote statements perfectly that defend your case, your recall of what actually happened becomes hazy. Your propaganda has polluted your own memory.

You gradually alienate yourself from all unwilling to carry your banner.
You demand that others take your side and be willing to get involved at some level. Unwillingness to do so brings friendship and loyalty into question.

You become willing to question God's motives, intentions, and care.
This is the most heartbreaking and self-degrading result of your state. If God was for you, if God could see better, if God was more concerned about the truth—he'd do something on your behalf by now! The only conclusion you can eventually draw is that he's defending the case of your enemy. "Fine. You'll see you were wrong! I'll fight this by myself." Worship is bluffed at best. You don't speak to God much now, except to bark out questions about his actions.

NOTES

UNREPENTANCE

When we have hurt someone else and are unwilling to repent, the process can look surprisingly similar:

You devalue the impact of your actions on the other person.

You have a subtle nagging feeling that if you admit you were wrong and apologize, you will lose the control you currently have in the circumstance. You believe you cannot afford this loss.

You wish the other person were more realistic and more mature. Then they would realize people get hurt all the time, and that since you're a good person, you didn't intend to hurt them.

You withdraw emotionally, physically, or both from the person you hurt.

You seek to defend yourself to those who know both you and the one you hurt by telling "your truth," but it is a distorted truth that aims to protect your image, your reputation, or your institution.

You become unable to see from any other vantage points but your own.

You become insensitive to your own misbehavior, while becoming hypersensitive to the misbehaviors of others.

You hear and dismiss the Spirit's offer to let you reflect on the consequences of your actions on the one you hurt, consequences which are often more devastating than your actions.

You become progressively more unhealthy, causing you to be overbearing, uncompassionate, calloused, bitter, and angry.

You gradually alienate yourself from all unwilling to carry your banner.

You move on to other friends or even other communities, leaving the past conflict behind.

You grow distant from God and lose intimacy with Jesus as you reject the gift of repentance he died to offer you.

SCRIPTURE

Romans 8:37-39 (NIV)

"No, in all these things we are more than conquerors through him who loved us. For I am convinced that neither death nor life, neither angels nor demons, neither the present nor the future, nor any powers, neither height nor depth, nor anything else in all creation, will be able to separate us from the love of God that is in Christ Jesus our Lord."

NOTES

REFLECTION QUESTIONS

What stages stood out the most to you for refusing to forgive? Why?

What stages stood out the most to you for refusing to repent? Why?

NOTES

Have you been on the receiving end of either of these cycles, or watched them as a bystanding friend? What was that like?

SECTION 5

In the Old and New Testament, writers expressed repeatedly that God stands against the proud but loves to give grace to the humble. James 4:6 (NIV) tells us, "But he gives us more grace. That is why Scripture says:

'God opposes the proud
but shows favor to the humble.'"

We can almost picture God sitting on his hands, waiting until we give up so he can rescue us. This is the collateral damage of our choice to refuse his gift of forgiveness. We become proud. The pattern laid out in the previous section is simply a person's pride being revealed. If humility is "trusting God and others with me," then the proud are those who are untrusting and self-protective. God works to move us to a place of humility, where we can experience freedom.

Unfortunately, the "healing" many of us have been taught is far from heartfelt. It isn't healing at all. It is the result of white-knuckling our way to forgiveness through reciting the right words with no change of heart. We don't trust that healing at all. We know God wants us to forgive. What we can't figure out is why we can only do it superficially, or why we reject it altogether as a hypocritical gesture when the other hasn't repented.

The goal of this study is to give us a way of seeing forgiveness, releasing us from being judge and jury or the relentless detectives rooting out clues and holes in stories. Nothing is more exhausting than refusing to forgive.

If we're to be set free, we must first embrace a forgiveness that is solely for our benefit. Only then can we extend forgiveness to the benefit of another. Until we understand the distinction, we can only conjure an external expression of forgiveness. Inside we'll continue seething, our hurt and thirst for revenge buried alive.

The way home is not the expected route. We assume life will be right when everyone apologizes long enough and completely enough to us, in public, perhaps through a televised worldwide event. Justice will be served when we are vindicated, proven right, publicly honored, and all damaging consequences are rectified.

That route home will never truly free us or give us what we hunger for. That route takes us deep into the desert, where there is no water and no life.

The first condition of returning home is that we must be weary enough. We must be weakened to the point we drop our defenses long enough to look to God and call out, "Help!" This condition is called repentance. Now, we may be saying, "What? Repentance? Are you kidding me? I didn't do anything. I'm the victim, remember?" Remember the tragedy of not trusting forgiveness? We've carried bitterness and have chosen to ignore God's protection and go it alone. And often, in the subjectivity of our inflamed and wounded bitterness, we become blinded to our part in the issue. Our hurt has given us permission to absolve ourselves of all wrongdoing. Repentance is God's antidote to the guilt we feel for both of these wrongs. We must face, maybe with the help of someone we trust, the brutal honesty of an accurate assessment of our role in this.

It's important to remember that this repentance is not the "man-up" religious bluffing we've tried before. Repentance isn't doing something about our sin. It is admitting we can't do anything about our sin. It is trusting that only God can cleanse us, and only He can convince us we're truly cleansed.

We've been told repentance is a promise to God that "I'm going to stop this sin," and "I'm sorry and I won't do it again," and "This time I mean it."

We mistake repentance for remorse. The intention not to sin is not the same as the power not to sin.

What if repentance wasn't a promise from you to God but a gift from God to you?

Scripture calls repentance a gift in 2 Timothy 2:25 (NASB) " . . . perhaps God may grant them repentance leading to the knowledge of the truth," and Acts 11:17-18, "'So if God gave them the same gift as he gave us, who believed in the Lord Jesus Christ, who was I to think that I could oppose God?' When they heard this, they had no further objections and praised God, saying, 'So then, God has granted even the Gentiles repentance unto life.'" It's not something we drum up, but the gifted ability to find ourselves saying, "God, I can't. You can. I trust You!" "God, I am trusting what You did for me on that cross to cleanse me of what I've done." This is called redemption: to liberate by payment, to release from debt or blame. Sin is resolved when we are cleansed of it. No amount of promises, amends, or right behavior can cleanse us. We are cleansed when we depend on the power of what Jesus did for us on the cross.

SCRIPTURE

1 John 1:7 (ESV)

"But if we walk in the light, as he is in the light, we have fellowship with one another, and the blood of Jesus his Son cleanses us from all sin."

NOTES

REFLECTION QUESTIONS

"What if repentance wasn't a promise from you to God but a gift from God to you?" How have you viewed repentance in the past? Is this different?

Have you ever held on to a hurt until you were publicly proven "right"? What happened in the meantime?

Turning to God for repentance and forgiveness requires humility. What emotions do you experience when you imagine turning to God for this instead of your own willpower?

NOTES

WEEK 2

God's Gift of Healing

MEETING TOGETHER

This week, we will hear from a couple about their experience with a broken relationship, and specifically how shame magnified their hurt and guilt. We will also hear what the journey of forgiveness and repentance looked like for them, and how Jesus met them in the middle of their broken relationship.

Galatians 2:20 (NIV)

"I have been crucified with Christ and I no longer live, but Christ lives in me. The life I now live in the body, I live by faith in the Son of God, who loved me and gave himself for me."

CONNECT

 25% OF YOUR TIME

AS A GROUP:

- Pray to open this time together. Who wants to volunteer?

- Connect question:

  » What is one of your favorite memories from your childhood?

- Check in questions:

  » What stood out to you this week, either from our conversation last time or the Digging Deeper material?

  » Last week we talked about practical, tangible ways we could invite God into our broken relationships. How did that play out this week?

LEARN

 25% OF YOUR TIME

>  **WATCH THE *STORY* VIDEO.**
> Find at ***trueface.org/HealingRelationshipsStudy.***

LIVE

50% OF YOUR TIME (HALF OF THE TIME DISCUSSING, HALF OF THE TIME APPLYING.)

DISCUSS:

What does this mean to me?

Choose a few questions that jump out to you from the list on the following page and process them as a group. Do your best to not give the answer you think you're supposed to—try to be as authentic and real as you can.

1 What stood out to you about Vic and Monique's story?

2 Where did you see shame driving their actions?

3 Vic had to give up control before he was able to move forward. Why do you think that is?

4 When have you seen God use someone else in your life to help you heal?

5 How does it change our experience when we see forgiveness and repentance as miraculous tools of healing, rather than something we grit our teeth and do?

6 As you consider repentance and forgiveness in your own life, what are some of the "yeah, but . . . " statements that go through your mind? For example, "Yeah, but they are just going to do it again," or, "Yeah, but they are overreacting." These might be legitimate concerns. Voice them with your group.

7 How does the way we view our identity change how we respond to shame?

APPLY:

What faith step is God inviting me to take?

We aren't called to step into forgiveness and repentance alone—Jesus wants to walk with us and empower us with the Spirit every step of the way. Move your group discussion towards how we can experience Jesus's closeness by asking the following questions.

WEEK 2: GOD'S GIFT OF HEALING

- How would your life look different if you experienced forgiveness and repentance as a miraculous gift in your life? What stops you from experiencing this?

- In this coming week's Digging Deeper material, we're going to explore how healing has an order of events. First, we experience healing between us and God, and then we experience healing between us and the other person. What is one practical, tangible way that you can begin experiencing healing with Jesus this week? Ideas to get you started:

  » Start the conversation with Jesus about the relationships in which you want to experience healing. Don't try to fix it—just allow Jesus to sit with you as you tell him all about your experience.

  » Ask a trusted friend or family member to help you walk through the steps outlined in Digging Deeper 2 as you process your hurt or guilt between you and God.

  » Notice what happens in your body as you think about trying to force yourself to forgive or repent when your heart isn't in it. Then, imagine receiving forgiveness or repentance as a miraculous gift from God that you can offer to others. Notice what happens in your body. Write down your observations.

» Write a letter to the Father about your hurt or your guilt. Include all the details, your emotions, and any consequences that have come after the event. Imagine God reading this letter with unending empathy and compassion. Then, trust him to take care of the situation. See Digging Deeper 2 for more guidance.

» Anything else come to mind? Be creative, but practical. Try to make it an actionable step in order to help integrate your actions with your beliefs.

• How I'm going to live it out:

• How can the group or one member in the group come alongside you in this?

PRAY TO CLOSE OUT THIS TIME TOGETHER.

NOTES

02

DIGGING DEEPER

Between now and your next meeting, read these five sections and reflect on the questions at the end. You can do them all at once, but we suggest breaking the five sections over multiple days to give yourself more processing time. This week we will be exploring vertical healing between us and God.

If you aren't able to go through the five sections before your next meeting, **that's okay.** Don't let it stop you from connecting with your community.

PASSAGE FOR THE WEEK

Ephesians 1:7-8 (NLT)

"He is so rich in kindness and grace that he purchased our freedom with the blood of his Son and forgave our sins. He has showered his kindness on us, along with all wisdom and understanding."

SECTION 1

Many of us have been taught that healing happens when we just mean it enough, are obedient enough, or say the right words. We try to force ourselves to feel repentant or forgiving and wonder why we can't seem to get our hearts on board. This is because most of us haven't been taught that healing has an order. First we must experience healing between us and God, and *then* we experience it between us and another.

We call the first step vertical healing. This is where we receive forgiveness from God if we have sinned and where we trust God to take care of our hurt if we have been sinned against. In vertical healing we allow the sin to move out of our control and into God's control. We release our stranglehold on the situation, trusting that God will carry us through.

We've been given the password that lets us move toward healing: "humility." That means trusting that God is with us and for us, absolutely and completely able, never making any mistakes in moving us forward.

He is fully sovereign. He loves us more than we love ourselves, and absolutely nothing can damage his total and complete control! He never messes up when it comes to you and me. We trust that even the worst events this life can bring are being used by God, who is molding and forging them into good. At this point, many of us have been told that because of what Jesus did for us we should just let go of our rights, stuff our feelings, and get back to living for God. Such theology would have to improve to reach heresy.

God never tells us to get over something and just get past it. Never. Instead, he asks us to trust him with every circumstance. This involves communicating with him honestly and in detail until we're sure we've left nothing out. He wants to hear it all. He wants to enter into every tear, every detail. He's been waiting for this moment. He's watched us go it alone. Now he will sit, elbows on knees, hands on chin, listening to every single word. We must sigh, cry, shout, or groan until he's certain we're done and that we've gotten it all out.

SCRIPTURE

1 Peter 5:7 (NIV)

"Cast all your anxiety on him because he cares for you."

NOTES

REFLECTION QUESTIONS

Have you experienced vertical healing—healing between you and God—before you have experienced healing between you and another person? What was that like?

"God never tells us to get over something and just get past it. Instead, he asks us to trust him with every circumstance." What comes up for you when you read this?

NOTES

SECTION 2

Now we will explore the steps of healing. This isn't a formula, and we may go back and forth between steps many times. This is a guide to help you process through your hurt or guilt with God, and maybe with a trusted friend. For each step there is a description of what you may feel like when you are seeking to forgive, and what you may feel like when you are seeking repentance. Many times, we are experiencing both.

You admit something happened.

God's provision for our healing always begins with recognizing that someone has sinned against us or we have sinned against someone else.

Forgiveness: If you have been hurt, you may be tempted to skip this step for a variety of reasons. If you were sinned against as a child—abused, neglected, or demeaned—you may not even remember or realize what happened. You think if you don't admit your pain, no one will have control over you. Someone more articulate or powerful will not be able to manipulate you into believing you're the guilty party. Or perhaps you want to deny that you have been hurt as a sign of your spiritual maturity: "This shouldn't bother me. I'll just move on."

But you cannot forgive until you admit you've been sinned against. This is an invitation to stop hiding the sin someone else has committed against you. To forgive, you must admit what is already true.

Repentance: If you have hurt someone else, you are prone to skip this step for very similar reasons to the one who's been hurt. You may have rationalized that the other person "shouldn't feel hurt," and admitting you hurt them feels like giving in. Sometimes you fear losing control of the relationships by admitting your actions and think if you just ignore it you can stay above the consequences. Shame is often holding you hostage, telling you if you truly acknowledge what happened it will prove you're a monster.

You cannot receive the gift of repentance —and then forgiveness—if you won't genuinely acknowledge what happened. A key here is that you need to admit the reality that your actions and inactions resulted in another person feeling hurt. Once you admit this reality, then you have the opportunity to turn from those actions to repentance.

SCRIPTURE

Ephesians 4:25 (NIV)

"Therefore each of you must put off falsehood and speak truthfully to your neighbor, for we are all members of one body."

NOTES

REFLECT

Enter into this step. Admit that something happened
that needs your and God's attention, whether you
have been hurt or you have hurt another.

NOTES

SECTION 3

You get in touch with the consequences of the act done against you or against another.

The consequences of sin are usually worse—sometimes far worse—than the sin itself, both for the one that was hurt and the one that hurt another. Sin grows over time, covering more area and gaining in power as it goes. While something might have seemed small to begin with, it may have expanded far and wide over time.

NOTES

Forgiveness: In order to understand the effect a sin has had on you, you need to connect with how that event is impacting your daily life. Have you experienced shame? Have you become fearful? Have you felt demeaned or devalued? Were you manipulated or shunned? Were there relational effects? Did you lose credibility or access with friends? Was your marriage affected? Did it impact your relationship with your children or people you work with? Did it affect your job, your income, or your future? Did you lose your position or influence? Has this changed how you see yourself or your attitude towards love, trust, friendship . . . or even God?

This is hard work. Often, it is more difficult to forgive another for the consequences of their sin than it is for the sin itself. To understand the consequences of the sin, you have to allow yourself to feel the pain of your responses. This work is sacred though. Harboring anger enables the sin that was committed against you to define you. No more! Remember, unresolved sins are buried alive, even the ones carried out against us. You must take your time. God is there, nodding and smiling at the courage coming from your trust in Him. This hard work prepares you to forgive.

Repentance: Getting in touch with the consequences of your sin can be very challenging if you are repenting for a variety of reasons. First, you may still be struggling with understanding why the other person felt hurt. You may argue that you wouldn't have felt hurt in that situation, that they're overreacting, or that they're trying to control you with their pain. These might even be valid concerns. But by the wonderful grace of God, you do not need to understand or even agree with the other person's pain to feel remorse for it. You can experience genuine, heartfelt repentance for how your actions or inactions resulted in another feeling hurt. Even if you never intended for your choices to hurt another, you can be deeply sorry that they did. For example, say you completely forgot that you agreed to meet a friend for lunch and stood them up. They now feel hurt, rejected, and unimportant in your life. That was not your intention or motive! But it is still the effect of your choices.

The second reason repentance is challenging is that you likely do not know all of the consequences of your actions. Between you and God, right now, you can enter into the consequences you know about and experience remorse for them. However, in a future step, you will need to invite the other person to share the consequences you don't know about if they are willing.

And finally, it can be very challenging and extremely important to acknowledge the consequences that have happened in your own life and ways you have been hurt in the other person's response. As the saying goes, "Hurt people hurt people." It's important that you explore the consequences of the event in your own life—both consequences from your own sin and from the sin done against you.

SCRIPTURE

Galatians 6:7-8 (NLT)

"Don't be misled—you cannot mock the justice of God. You will always harvest what you plant. Those who live only to satisfy their own sinful nature will harvest decay and death from that sinful nature. But those who live to please the Spirit will harvest everlasting life from the Spirit."

REFLECT

Take time to tell God about the consequences of what happened and ask him to help you explore them. The consequences of sin are often more difficult to heal from than the sin itself, and it's okay if you need to return to this step many times as you discover more consequences.

NOTES

SECTION 4

You tell God what happened.

Forgiveness: Now it's time to pour out your heart, telling him as best you can exactly what has happened.

Your old programming tells you he doesn't want to hear it. You might think, "No way! This is for over-emotional people. I don't do that stuff." You might think any rehearsal of the event is akin to wallowing in it. You are wrong.

You must excavate every effect and emotion you've buried about the sin against you. Every last bit. This is the mysterious, beautiful part of your interaction with God. It is reclaiming this truth of your relationship: "You care even more deeply and fully than I do. Enter into this." For the first time in a long time, you feel heard, known, validated, and safe.

Repentance: Now you get to tell the whole story of what happened. You show it all to God: all your defenses, your reasoning, what you know of the consequences for the other person, what you know of the consequences for yourself. You allow him to enter into your confused, upset heart and all the accompanying emotions. You express your feelings of guilt, confusion, anger, shame, hurt, or whatever else.

You allow God to see it all, even your worst, petty defenses and explanations. You must continue until you feel sure he's heard your side and your experience—until you know that the Father fully understands what happened for you. At this point, you can begin to lay down your defenses, trusting that God is your defender and that in him you're safe to own your sin.

SCRIPTURE

Psalm 18:1-2 (NLT)

"I love you, Lord;
*   you are my strength.*
The Lord is my rock, my fortress, and my savior;
*   my God is my rock, in whom I find protection.*
He is my shield, the power that saves me,
*   and my place of safety."*

REFLECT

Take a long walk or shut your phone off for an hour or pull out a sheet of paper, and begin writing down your story. Tell God everything that happened. Make sure that there's nothing left unsaid, unexplained, unexpressed, until you're sure God has heard, seen, and entered into it all.

NOTES

SECTION 5

You forgive the offender or you repent, for your benefit.

Forgiveness: Wait ... for your benefit?

Yes.

This section describes the missing piece in why forgiveness has not taken root in many of us. Forgiving between you and God is one of the most freeing, healing, practical expressions of God's power you can experience on this side of heaven. God frees your heart, eventually leading you to free the one who's hurt you, and that process is central to God's deepest will and intentions.

Forgiveness has an order. You must initiate the vertical transaction with God before you can move into the horizontal transaction with another. First, before God, you forgive the offender(s) for what they've done and the consequences they've brought into your life. This is before you and God, and it is for your sake. It does not let anyone off the hook; it does not excuse any action. It does not restore *relational* forgiveness to the other. This is the vertical transaction. It is a choice to free yourself, to begin healing.

Trusting God's character, strength, love, and protection, you place the entire list of consequences and loss into his hands. This is a big decision. It's a scary, beautiful, overwhelming moment of trust.

NOTES

You actually imagine removing every effect of that sin and placing it onto God. You hand over everything. You trust God will not mock you, ignore you, or forget your pain. You trust he will protect you and defend your heart, bringing beauty out of hurt. You trust he will cleanse you as he promised.

You are giving up your rights to decide what is best for that person or yourself. You're handing the case over to the only judge who can see the entire story and who loves both the offender and the victim perfectly. This is a unique moment when faith becomes a risked action. You're putting everything on the line because, after all, this is your life, your pain, your reputation. Never is the proof of new life more evident than when you cede control because of your trust in God's character, love, and power. Then the whole incident moves out of your sphere and into God's.

Only then will you be freed to go to your offender and forgive him. If you don't get this right—if you attempt to forgive, unclean before God—you move toward your offender in veiled bitterness, judgment, and a spirit of retribution. You bring the residue of unresolved sin into the equation, and everyone can smell it.

If you say, "I'm not going to forgive until he repents," you end up in resentment. In your unwillingness to forgive before God, you become the issue.

The question then is, how do you know you've actually forgiven someone who's sinned against you? Answer: The moment you can offer that person your love again. When forgiveness stays only in your mind as a formula or technique, it doesn't sink deep into your heart.

When you choose to let go, to forgive vertically before God, it's like huge cement bags have been lifted off your shoulders. It's like coming out of a moldy basement with a cement floor and suddenly breathing ocean air on the sand at Big Sur. It feels like being home.

Repentance: Repentance always begins between you and God. Remember what we learned in Digging Deeper 1? Repentance is not a promise from you to God, but a gift from God to you. You can do nothing—absolutely nothing—to make provision for your sin. In repentance you depend on God to work a miracle, to turn water into wine. You trust him with your very self—with your actions and their consequences.

Here, you trust that God's love for you is unchanging regardless of your behavior. You trust that he truly has made you into a new creation, a holy and beloved saint—who still sins. You trust that he alone can cleanse you of this sin and the shame that comes with it. Jesus died to give you freedom from your sins, including this most recent one, but he also died to free you from your shame, giving you a new, shame-free identity. He stands with his hands out, waiting for you to hand him your sin, your shame, and all their consequences. His gaze is steady with delight, love, and grace. In repentance, you receive that gift of being cleansed, and you allow him to remind you of

NOTES

who you truly are in him. This is sacred, mystical work. This is a miracle.

When you are settled in God's deep, abiding love for you and his all-encompassing forgiveness, you are ready to go to another and fully own your actions and their consequences. You no longer have to defend, explain, and deflect. Your identity is not on the line. This latest misstep does not prove you are unlovable. Indeed, when you receive forgiveness and cleansing from the Father, you are able to offer your love and affection to the one you have hurt in an entirely new way.

SCRIPTURE

1 John 1:9 (NIV)

"If we confess our sins, he is faithful and just and will forgive us our sins and purify us from all unrighteousness."

NOTES

REFLECT

Walk through these steps, either for forgiveness, repentance, or—depending on the situation—both. Feel free to revisit some of the other steps. Don't force it. Remember, Jesus is offering this gift of healing out of his extravagant grace. It's not something you can drum up or willpower your way into. This is deep work, but life-giving freedom is waiting on the other side.

NOTES

WEEK 3

Healing Starts with Me and God

MEETING TOGETHER

God has designed these two pathways, forgiveness and repentance, to lead us back into relationship with him and with others. This week we get to explore some of what scripture says about this process of healing.

Mark 1:14 (NIV)

"After John was put in prison, Jesus went into Galilee, proclaiming the good news of God. 'The time has come,' he said. 'The kingdom of God has come near. Repent and believe the good news!'"

CONNECT

🕐 **20% OF YOUR TIME**

- Pray to open this time together. Who wants to volunteer?

- Connect question:

  » What's been one struggle or low point in your week? What's been one highlight?

- Check in questions:

  » Last week we talked about practical, tangible ways that we can start experiencing healing with Jesus. How did that play out this past week? If you didn't take the step you chose last week, what do you think held you back?

» What stood out to you this week, either from our conversation last time or the Digging Deeper material?

LEARN

 **20% OF YOUR TIME**

- First, have someone read Romans 12:2-3 out loud for the group. The ESV version is below.

SCRIPTURE:

Romans 12:2-3 (ESV)

"Do not be conformed to this world, but be transformed by the renewal of your mind, that by testing you may discern what is the will of God, what is good and acceptable and perfect. For by the grace given to me I say to everyone among you not to think of himself more highly than he ought to think, but to think with sober judgment, each according to the measure of faith that God has assigned."

 THEN, WATCH THE *STUDY* VIDEO.
Find at *trueface.org/HealingRelationshipsStudy.*

NOTES

LIVE

 60% OF YOUR TIME

TIME OF REFLECTION:

Spend five minutes in silence to contemplate the two
words Carson shared with us. What do these mean
for you? Where do you sense a need for them in
your own life?

χάρις, *charis*: grace, a surprise gift

μετάνοια, *metanoia*: repentance, changing one's mind
about someone or something, rethinking

DISCUSS:

What does this mean to me?

Choose a few questions that jump out to you from the list below and process them as a group.

1 What stood out to you from the video?

2 Forgiveness and repentance are two sides of the same coin. Which do you struggle with the most? What does that look like?

3 Where in your life do you connect with Carson's phrase, "Sometimes we don't want grace. We want to work for it."

4 Where have you struggled to forgive yourself?

5 How does viewing repentance as a gift for reconciling a relationship differ from your previous view of repentance?

6 "I'm going to choose to believe what he says about me, not my own thoughts." How does this change your experience of forgiveness and repentance?

7 What stops you from experiencing repentance in your own life? What stops you from experiencing forgiveness in your own life?

NOTES

APPLY:

What faith step is God inviting me to take?

We all have areas that we need to experience healing in. We need this freeing, powerful gift of repentance—including repenting from refusing to forgive one another. If you are comfortable and feel safe, share with the group an area of your life where you want to experience repentance and forgiveness.

What is one actionable step that you can take toward repentance and forgiveness with God this next week?

NOTES

How can the group encourage you and come alongside you in this?

 TIP: *this may be a good time to break into smaller groups of two or three and spend time praying together.*

PRAY TO CLOSE OUT THIS TIME TOGETHER.

DIGGING DEEPER

Between now and when you next meet together, read these five sections and reflect on the questions at the end. You can do them all at once, but we suggest breaking the five sections over multiple days to give yourself more processing time. This week, we will be exploring horizontal healing with another.

If you aren't able to go through the five sections before your next meeting, **that's okay**. Don't let it stop you from connecting with your community.

PASSAGE FOR THE WEEK

Matthew 5:23-24 (NIV)

*"Therefore, if you are offering your gift at the altar
and there, remember that your brother or sister has
something against you, leave your gift there in front of
the altar. First go and be reconciled to them; then come
and offer your gift."*

SECTION 1

Healing begins between you and God with vertical
healing. In vertical healing, you entrust the situation
to God and receive his peace and healing. You allow
the love of Christ to wash over your shame, reminding
you that you are a beloved child and a holy saint, fully
accepted and enjoyed.

From this place of security and love, you move into
horizontal healing. This is when you pursue healing
between you and another, either extending them the
marvelous gift of forgiveness that God has given you
or by wholeheartedly repenting for the ways you have
hurt another person—or, perhaps most commonly,
both. In many situations, especially if you have let sin
fester, you find yourself in a complicated tangle of
both hurt and guilt, wounding and wounds. Thankfully,
God's gracious salve of healing can be applied to all.

This horizontal healing will rarely go the way you
expect. It may take more time than you want it to. The

NOTES

other person may not be ready to own their part or start the conversation. This is one of the many reasons vertical forgiveness is so incredible: it allows you to experience the freedom and peace of healing, even if the one you hurt or the one who hurt you is unwilling to come to the table. You are responsible for your side of the equation and for pursuing healing, and you cannot force anyone to be ready to engage with you.

Stepping out into horizontal healing takes great courage and is a move against the dominion of darkness that wants to keep us isolated, wounded, and bitter. This week we will explore what it looks like to reach out to someone we want to experience healing with, to offer them our hearts, and to stand with the King of Love and Reconciliation.

SCRIPTURE

Romans 12:18 (NIV)

"If it is possible, as far as it depends on you, live at peace with everyone."

NOTES

REFLECTION QUESTIONS

Is vertical healing or horizontal healing more uncomfortable for you? Why?

As you think about having a conversation with someone you'd like to experience healing with, what concerns or fears come up?

NOTES

SECTION 2

I engage with the other person.

Forgiveness: If you have been hurt by someone, do they know they have hurt you? Have you risked vulnerability in telling them how their actions affected you? Too often one person is hurt and the other has no idea. Now that you have experienced forgiving the other person between you and God, you can approach them and share how you have been feeling.

Then, you tell the offender you've forgiven them when they repent for their sake. To declare "I forgive you" before a person has the opportunity to repent robs the offender of the opportunity for their own life-freeing repentance. God uses repentance to heal guilty hearts, and premature forgiveness will not free the other person from their offense or heal the relationship. The one who sinned against you must repent for their sake to be healed from that sin.

This is not a smooth or exact interaction. And it is important to note that it may not be safe to approach or engage with the one that hurt you, depending on the circumstances. Or, you may need support in engaging, such as a mediator, trusted mentor, or counselor. It can take many conversations over a long period of time to restore a relationship in truth and beauty. But a relationship restored through repentance is often stronger, healthier, and more faithful than it was before.

NOTES

You can pursue reconciliation, but you can't force it. You can't demand repentance. Repentance requires trusting God's work. Insistence and $3.50 will get you a small latte and nothing more.

If your offender repents, you forgive with the goal of restoring the relationship, not just resolving a conflict. You desire their repentance, but not so that you can hold it over them. You want it so that you can move on in mutual trust and love. Their repentance will not heal your heart. **That healing began when you forgave them before God. Their repentance will begin to heal your *relationship.*** As you forgive your offender for their sake, it prepares the way for the relationship to be restored.

Isn't that incredible? When you allow God to heal you from being sinned against, you get to turn around and help those who've sinned against you in healing their sin. It's a beautiful process.

Repentance: If you are repenting to someone you have hurt, you now get to start the conversation with them. You can invite them for coffee, ask to talk on the phone, or go for a walk. You share with them the guilt you've been carrying, and the actions and consequences you know of. You can ask them if they are willing to share with you what you don't know— what consequences and effects they have experienced from your action or inaction that you are unaware of.

If they are willing to open up to you, you need to remember: you are loved and enjoyed and accepted by God, even as you face the effects of your sin. You can enter into their pain, because you know it does not change your identity. You are a holy saint—who still sins, hurts others, and has rough edges that will take a lifetime of maturing.

Now you can repent of the things they have shared. You can offer heartfelt regret and repentance for how your actions—intentional or not—hurt them. And you can ask if they are willing to forgive you. They might not be willing to. They may not be ready. That's okay. You have been freed before God, and now you get to offer repentance and healing. The rest is left to their process and God's timing as he works in their hearts. Regardless of where they are, you get to experience the freedom and peace of owning your sin and its influence.

NOTES

SCRIPTURE

Ephesians 4:31-32 (NIV)

"Get rid of all bitterness, rage and anger, brawling and slander, along with every form of malice. Be kind and compassionate to one another, forgiving each other, just as in Christ God forgave you."

REFLECTION QUESTIONS

What are your biggest barriers to engaging with the person you have hurt or have been hurt by?

How and when will you start this conversation? Who can encourage you to follow through on this?

NOTES

SECTION 3

I distinguish between forgiveness and trust.

Forgiveness: Forgiveness does not demand that you now fully trust the other person. This misunderstanding causes many of us to balk at forgiveness. Because you can't trust a person, you believe you can't forgive them. Forgiveness and trust are separate issues. Even if you've forgiven your offender—even if your offender has repented and asked for forgiveness—you will still have to deal with the issue of mutual trust. Your expectations must be realistic, because while trust is easily broken, it is recovered very slowly. Sometimes it never recovers. Forgiveness carries the hope of renewed trust, but it offers no mandate or guarantee. Once you've risked baring your throat in pursuing forgiveness, trust longs to follow. From here, it is a matter of time, opportunity, and an open heart.

Repentance: Just because the other person has truly forgiven you does not mean that all the effects of the hurt are undone. One of the most painful consequences of sin is broken trust. The road back to trust is incredibly diverse—long or short, winding or straight, with sudden left turns or simply longer than you had hoped. It might not happen. There are no guarantees for how this story will go. You cannot make them trust you, but you can consistently offer connection. You can be trustworthy in the small things as they learn to trust you again in the bigger things. You can be open to honest conversations about where each of you are in life and in your relationship.

SCRIPTURE

Romans 15:5-7 (NIV)

"May the God who gives endurance and encouragement give you the same attitude of mind toward each other that Christ Jesus had, so that with one mind and one voice you may glorify the God and Father of our Lord Jesus Christ. Accept one another, then, just as Christ accepted you, in order to bring praise to God."

REFLECTION QUESTIONS

Where have you experienced broken trust in your life?

How do you usually respond to breaking someone else's trust? To having your trust broken?

25

SECTION 4

When possible, you seek reconciliation, not just conflict resolution.

Forgiveness & Repentance: Sometimes in your shame and self-protection you want to get past the issue and leave the relationship to die. Your effort will be to resolve a conflict rather than reconcile a relationship. That way you imagine you can get past the ugliness and pain in your heart without letting go of your disdain and rigid resentment toward the other person. This seems honorable, but the difference between resolution and reconciliation is like the difference between fluorescent lights and a stunning sunrise.

When you give the other an opportunity to ask, "Will you forgive me?" you give the gift of engaging in the relationship. Repentance and forgiveness are not a means to fix your behavior. They are gifts of grace to heal your relationships. Reconciliation belongs in a completely different stratosphere than mere conflict resolution. When you want to "fix" a conflict, you will use terms like, "I'm sorry that happened," or "I really made a big mistake on that one." When you're willing to say, "Will you forgive me because I did_____?" you create an opportunity for the other person to forgive you and enter back into a heart relationship with you.

In your eagerness to fix conflicts, you can push people to apologize. But no one stays "fixed" when you force the issue. You can say "I'm sorry," but sometimes those are just words. Nothing has been reconciled. You're left each defending your turf and still just as resentful, even if the "right" words have been spoken.

Grace always invites rather than demands reconciliation. An apology may push the issue away for the moment, but it won't heal a relationship and it rarely solves any issue. The courage to refuse quick fixes and to engage long and vulnerably enough to woo honest, humble reconciliation from the depths of our new heart . . . this is the work of human beings loving with the love of Jesus.

Sometimes reconciliation is not possible or is not safe. You may be healing from traumatic and abusive relationships in which entering back into a relationship with the offender is unwise and impossible. Your physical, mental, emotional, and spiritual safety needs to be carefully considered. And sometimes you are not able to pursue reconciliation now, but the Lord may open the door for it in the future.

You need to realize that just because you follow Jesus does not mean you live in a pretend fantasyland where everyone is happy and at peace all the time. You can still hurt, fail, and bear jealousy toward others—and they can do the same to you. The difference is in what you are learning to believe: that Jesus lives in you and that you are in Jesus. You are actually righteous, delighted in, and without condemnation even when you do fail. You get to believe this for the other Jesus followers in your life too. Over time you actually mature into who God says you are, and you stop hurting each other as often. Slowly, the world around you transforms into a place of safety, trust, freedom, and love better than you could dream.

SCRIPTURE

2 Corinthians 13:11 (NIV)

"Finally, brothers and sisters, rejoice! Strive for full restoration, encourage one another, be of one mind, live in peace. And the God of love and peace will be with you."

NOTES

REFLECTION QUESTIONS

What do you think about the statement, "Repentance and forgiveness are not a means to fix our behavior. They are gifts of grace to heal our relationships"?

What prevents you from reconciling a relationship?

Who have you experienced reconciliation with where it made your relationship stronger?

NOTES

SECTION 5

John 10:10 (ESV)

"The thief comes only to steal and kill and destroy. I came that they may have life and have it abundantly."

As we discussed at the very beginning of this study, we were made for relationships with God and with others. We were created to flourish in safe, real, authentic community, displaying the love and grace of God as we protect, encourage, comfort, and strengthen one another. It is not good for us to be alone.

The enemy knows this. This is why our relationships are a centerpiece of the war he wages—if he can break us apart and keep us apart, then he can stifle our outpouring of grace, justice, mercy, love, compassion, gentleness, wisdom, courage, and so much more. If he can isolate us, we aren't nearly as much of a threat.

The enemy is old and well-versed in our vices. He knows how to sow jealousy, pride, and discord among us. A hurt feeling here, a lash of anger there. And then he convinces us to let it rot inside of us. "It's not a big deal," we reason, "I'll just get over it." The enemy knows that that's not how sin works. If he can get us to ignore it, it will quietly widen the chasm between us. Break us apart and keep us apart—that's his battle plan.

Do you see this in your life, your family, your community, your nation? Are people being broken apart and kept apart? Are they unable to find common ground again after being hurt? Is it easier to retreat, isolate, cut off, demean, or ignore? Unfortunately, the enemy knows what he's doing.

But we serve the God of reconciliation, and by his grace that is not the end of the story! When we accepted Christ and he transformed us into New Kingdom Creations, we became agents of healing (even if we didn't know it). We have been transformed and given Christ's heart as our true heart—hearts of forgiveness and repentance. Jesus was always willing to forgive, whether it was Peter denying him, the thief next to him on the cross, or ultimately even those who betrayed and killed him. As we remember the definition of repentance, to turn from our will to God's, we see Jesus modeling this perfectly and constantly in his life. Even when he faced death and asked for another way, he remained steadfast in turning to God. "Not my will, but your will be done." We can trust that God will redeem our situation, but we also get to trust that through his miraculous work on the cross he is maturing us into the kind of people that naturally want to forgive and repent; it's in our very Christ-fused nature. Our flesh will try to convince us that this isn't true. It will try to convince us that we aren't truly new, Spirit-infused creations. However, as Paul says in Romans 8:9 (NLT), "But you are not controlled by your sinful nature. You are controlled by the Spirit if you have the Spirit of God living in you." Thanks to the Holy Spirit we have all of Christ's courage, love, and humility available to us every day, and we can stand against the powers of darkness that hope to break humans apart and keep them apart. We can reach out, reach across, forgive, repent, reconcile, and come back together.

So, will you stand? Will you step out against the enemy that wants to convince you to let that hurt or guilt fester? Will you reject isolation and fractured relationships and let Jesus lead you toward healing, wholeness, and true community?

SCRIPTURE

2 Corinthians 2:10-11 (NIV)

"Anyone you forgive, I also forgive. And what I have forgiven—if there was anything to forgive—I have forgiven in the sight of Christ for your sake, in order that Satan might not outwit us. For we are not unaware of his schemes."

NOTES

REFLECTION QUESTIONS

What would it look like in your own life, community, or country to pursue relational healing?

How does the enemy convince you to ignore relational healing? How can you stand against him?

WEEK 4

Healing Overflows to You and Me

NOTES

MEETING TOGETHER

This week we're going to look at how we can step out into horizontal healing and participate in Christ's ministry of reconciliation. Engaging in repentance and forgiveness with others can be messy and challenging, but thankfully we have a God who is a master navigator of these winding, beautiful roads.

2 Corinthians 5:18-19

"All this is from God, who reconciled us to himself through Christ and gave us the ministry of reconciliation: that God was reconciling the world to himself in Christ, not counting people's sins against them. And he has committed to us the message of reconciliation."

CONNECT

 30% OF YOUR TIME

AS A GROUP:

- Pray to begin this time together. Who wants to volunteer?

- Warm-up question:

  » What are you currently passionate about?

- Check-in questions:

  » What came up for you over the past week, either from our meeting together or from your Digging Deeper reading?

  » What is something that has stood out to you personally over the past four weeks?

LEARN

 20% OF YOUR TIME

> **WATCH THE *LIVE* VIDEO.**
> Find at ***trueface.org/HealingRelationshipsStudy.***

LIVE

50% OF YOUR TIME

DISCUSS:

What does this mean to me?

Choose a few questions that jump out at you from the list below to process as a group.

1 What stood out to you in the video?

2 What makes these forgiveness and repentance conversations so difficult for us?

NOTES

3 Why does a loving God desire for us to experience healing?

4 Which do you struggle more with: starting a conversation with someone you hurt or starting a conversation with someone who hurt you?

5 What motivates you to have that "boat-rocking, hard conversation"?

6 What would you need to trust God with in order to step out into horizontal healing?

7 How can we navigate having safe and healthy boundaries without using that as an excuse to avoid healing?

NOTES

PRACTICAL STEPS:

1. Seek the wisdom of the Holy Spirit in prayer.
2. Seek the counsel of a wise and trusted friend.
3. **Ask:** How can I love this person well in the conversation?

EXERCISE:

Spend five minutes individually processing the questions below.

1 Who do I want to experience healing with?

2 How could I trust God with my reservations or barriers?

3 Have I forgiven them vertically with God before moving to forgive them horizontally?

4 How can my group or trusted friends support and protect me as I move forward?

5 What would my hope be for this relationship?

NOTES

APPLY:

What faith step is God inviting me to take?

We can agree that healing is important and that God desires this for us and still not step out in faith in our own lives. When it comes to having a real conversation around an actual issue, we freeze. Here's where the rubber meets the road: how can you courageously step forward in healing with the other person this week? Talk about it practically and tangibly. Here are some ideas to get you started:

» Send a text to the person you'd like to experience healing with now, asking them if they could grab coffee or a drink in the next week.

» Journal your hurts, hopes, and forgiveness of the wrongs that have been done.

» Choose a time that you're going to call that person, and if they don't answer, decide when you'll call a second time. Decide if you'll leave a voicemail.

» Give someone you trust permission to help you reach out and to protect you from avoiding the situation.

» Set up a counseling appointment in the next two weeks for some professional guidance in healing or processing past pain.

NOTES

» Reach out to a trusted mentor, friend, leader, or pastor and ask them to meet with you and the other person if you feel a third party would be helpful.

» Anything else come to mind? Every situation is different and may require different steps.

- How I'm going to live it out:

- How can the group come alongside you, encourage you, and protect you as you pursue healing? What would feel loving to you as you take this step?

PRAY TO CLOSE OUT THIS TIME TOGETHER.

NOTES

DIGGING DEEPER

"Above all, love each other deeply, because love covers over a multitude of sins." **1 Peter 4:8 (NIV)**

God has designed each and every one of us for authentic relationships that can weather storms and heal fractures. Despite our best intentions, we're going to get hurt and we're going to hurt others. But God in his abounding grace has given us these miraculous gifts of forgiveness and repentance to heal and repair—often leading to relationships that are even stronger than before.

You were made to be a peace*maker*, to carry the banner of love and unity into a war that hopes for division and enmity. Follow the King into healing, freedom, and relational peace that passes worldly understanding.

If you're looking for more resources head to *Trueface.org.*

We have additional books, studies, and experiences to help you continue building high-trust communities of grace and inviting others to come and experience this life alongside you. You can also connect with thousands of others living the Trueface life on social media:

Instagram: @truefacelife

Facebook: @truefacecommunity

Twitter: @truefaced

CONTRIBUTORS

This study is based on *The Cure* by John Lynch, Bruce McNicol, and Bill Thrall, and contains source material from chapter five, "Two Healings." The executive editor and writer of this study was Brittany Sawrey.

ROBBY ANGLE

Robby Angle serves as the President and CEO of Trueface in Dawsonville, Georgia with his wife, Emily, and their eight children. Prior to Trueface, Robby served for over seven years at North Point Community Church in Atlanta, Georgia as the Director of Adult Ministry Environments and Director of Men's Groups. Robby led group counseling as a Licensed Professional Counselor and served with Samaritan's Purse in Pakistan and Myanmar overseeing international disaster response teams. Angle holds a certificate in biblical studies and degrees in business and counseling.

KEISHA CARTER-BROWN, LCSW

Keisha Carter Brown holds a master's degree in social work from Barry University in Miami, Florida. Prior to attending Barry University, Keisha completed her Bachelor of Arts in Human Development (with a minor in psychology) at Eckerd College. Keisha has continued her education by completing training in Holistic Nutrition as well as Health and Wellness to ultimately earn her certification as a Holistic Health Coach. As a LCSW, her therapeutic approach focuses on person-centered and empowerment-focused therapies. According to Keisha's view of counseling, the ultimate goal is to empower each client with the tools they need to improve their quality of life. Regarding Holistic Health coaching, Keisha believes that nutrition and lifestyle directly affect one's mood and overall mental health. Keisha lives and works in Cumming Georgia with her loving husband David Brown, super cool two-year-old son DK, and silly dog Valarie.

DR. CARSON PUE

Pue's more than three decades in high level leadership positions has prepared him well for speaking into the lives of today's leaders where he's in high demand through the organization he founded, Quadrant Leadership, Inc. Carson spends his time speaking, writing, consulting and providing executive mentoring to some of the top leaders in the business and non-profit world. Carson formerly served as director for Insight for Living/Canada, was Executive Minister for Vancouver's historic First Baptist Church as well as being the CEO of Arrow Leadership, a global organization dedicated to emerging and executive leadership development. Pue is also an internationally known keynote speaker and published bestselling author of *Mentoring Leaders: Wisdom for Developing Calling, Character and Competency* (Baker Books, 2005) which is in its 7th printing.

VIC AND MONIQUE WOODWARD

Vic and Monique Woodward are co-founders of Marriage Mosaic, which is a division of InFocus Ministries. They have been serving marriages for twenty years and have a vision for thriving marriages. Having walked through their own marriage crisis in 1997, they believe nothing is impossible with God. He has brought restoration, healing, and new found freedom. Marriage Mosaic seeks to build up marriages through premarital counsel, marriage workshops and retreats, mentoring, small groups, and developing a marriage mentor team. The Woodward's have been married for twenty-nine years and reside in Burlington, Washington. They have four adult children and four granddaughters. Along with marriage ministry and their family, they have a passion for the outdoors. Some of their marriage workshops are mobile, involving podcasts, scenic views/drives, great food and more!

ℳ TRUEFACE

SMALL GROUP STUDIES

EMBARK

Our resource for starting a transformational small group, *Embark* is the companion group guide to *The Cure for Groups*. Through videos, discussion questions, and practical group applications, it guides you in creating a small group that's bursting with life, depth, and the kind of authentic community Jesus created us for.

TWO ROADS

Explore the first three chapters of *The Cure* in-depth with this small group study. *Two Roads* is designed to help your group travel beyond the mask and start experiencing real, authentic relationships through videos, discussion questions, scripture, and application.

CRAZY-MAKING

Have you ever kept doing something you don't want to do? We all have these patterns in our lives that we just can't seem to shake. In this four-week study, you'll explore where these patterns come from, why we keep repeating them, and how to stop the crazy and live in the freedom Jesus made possible.

THE HEART OF MAN PARTICIPANT GUIDE

With contributions from Jackie Hill Perry, Dan Allender, WM Paul Young, Jay Stringer and John and Stasi Eldredge, this Trueface resource guides your group through unpacking and processing *The Heart of Man* movie and how to experience the love of the Father in the midst of our darkest struggles.

BOOKS

THE CURE

Unpacking our view of ourselves and our view of God, *The Cure* invites you to remove your mask and experience God's lavish grace. This flagship book explores identity, community, sin, healing, destiny, and more as you discover that maybe God isn't who you think he is . . . and neither are you.

THE CURE FOR GROUPS

Do you want the kind of small group people will talk about the rest of their lives? A practical guide to starting (or re-igniting) your group, *The Cure for Groups* unpacks five Core Components to build a group that's bursting with life, depth, and the kind of life-changing community Jesus modeled for us.

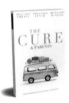

THE CURE AND PARENTS

Travel with the Clawson family on their summer vacation as they struggle to navigate their family dynamics. Told partly through narrative and partly through teaching, this resource is for anyone wanting to bring grace to their family.

TRUST FOR TODAY

This 365-day devotional invites you to experience grace in your daily life, both in the big moments and the details of life. Use these short readings to incorporate grace into your everyday.

BOOKS

BO'S CAFÉ

Steven Kerner is living the dream in southern California, until his wife kicks him out after another angry outburst. Walk with Steven and his eccentric mentor Andy as they explore Steven's unresolved problems and performance-based life, rediscovering the restoration and healing only God's grace can provide.

THE ASCENT OF A LEADER

Become the leader people want to follow by opening yourself up to the influences that develop character: enduring relationships with friends, family and God. *The Ascent of a Leader* guides you through cultivating extraordinary character in your home, company, community, and every other arena of life.

BEHIND THE MASK

When sin enters our lives, we have automatic, God-given responses. If we are the one who sinned, our response is guilt. If we are sinned against, our response is hurt. Explore these two involuntary responses and how they can lead to painful patterns of hiding and hurting, unless we allow the grace of Jesus to heal us.

NOTES

TRUEFACE

beyond the mask